Summary

Of

How Not To Die:

Discover the Foods Scientifically Proven to Prevent and Reverse Disease

By

Michael Greger MD

Copyright © 2017 Concise Reading

All rights reserved.

ISBN:

9781976836657

DEDICATION

For everyone who loves reading and books.

Whenever you read a good book, somewhere in the world a door opens to allow in more light. —Vera Nazarian

Table of Contents

Attention: Our Free Gift To You 1

Disclaimer 2

Summary of How Not To Die 4

    Preface 5

    INTRODUCTION: 7

    Preventing, Arresting and Reversing Our Leading Killers 7

    PART I 10

        CHAPTER 1: How Not to Die from Heart Disease 10

        CHAPTER 2: How Not to Die from Lung Diseases 12

        CHAPTER 3: How Not to Die from Brain Diseases 14

        CHAPTER 4: How Not to Die from Digestive Cancers 16

        CHAPTER 5: How Not to Die from Infections 18

        CHAPTER 6: How Not to Die from Diabetes 20

        CHAPTER 7: How Not to Die from High Blood Pressure 22

        CHAPTER 8: How Not to Die from Liver Diseases 24

        CHAPTER 9: How Not to Die from Blood Cancers 26

        CHAPTER 10: How Not to Die from Kidney Disease 28

        CHAPTER 11: How Not to Die from Breast Cancer 30

        CHAPTER 12: How Not to Die from Suicidal Depression 32

        CHAPTER 13: How Not to Die from Prostate Cancer 33

        CHAPTER 14: How Not to Die from Parkinson's Disease 34

        CHAPTER 15: How Not to Die from Iatrogenic Causes (or, How Not to Die from Doctors) 35

PART II	37
INTRODUCTION	37
Dr Greger's Daily Dozen	39
Conclusion	44
Background Information about How Not to Die	45
Background Information about Dr Michael Greger	48
Cover Questions	50
Trivia Questions about How Not to Die	51
Trivia Questions about Dr Michael Greger	52
Discussion Questions	53
Thank You	55

Attention: Our Free Gift To You

As a way to say "Thank You" for being a fan of our series, we have included a free gift for you.

To get your free gift, please visit:

http://www.concisereading.com/gift/

The Concise Reading Team

Disclaimer

Note to readers:

This is an unofficial summary & analysis of Dr Michael Greger's "How Not To Die: Discover the Foods Scientifically Proven to Prevent and Reverse Disease" designed to enrich your reading experience.

Disclaimer: All Rights Reserved. No part of this publication may be reproduced or retransmitted, electronic or mechanical, without the written permission of the publisher; with the exception of brief quotes used in connection in reviews written for inclusion in a magazine or newspaper.

This Book is licensed for your personal enjoyment only. This Book may not be re-sold or given away to other people. If you would like to share this book with another person, please purchase an additional copy for each recipient. If you're reading this book and did not purchase it, please purchase your own copy.

Product names, logos, brands, and other trademarks featured or referred to within this publication are the property of their respective trademark holders. These trademark holders are not affiliated with us and they do not sponsor or endorse our publications. This book is unofficial and unauthorized. It is not authorized, approved, licensed, or endorsed by the aforementioned interests or any of their licensees.

The information in this book has been provided for educational and entertainment purposes only.

The information contained in this book has been compiled from sources deemed reliable and it is accurate to the best of the Author's knowledge; however, the Author cannot guarantee its accuracy and validity and cannot be held liable for any errors or omissions. Upon using the information contained in this book, you agree to hold harmless the Author from and against any damages, costs, and expenses, including any legal fees, potentially resulting from the application of any of the information provided by this guide. The disclaimer applies to any damages or injury caused by the use and application, whether directly or indirectly, of any advice or information presented, whether for breach of contract, tort, neglect, personal injury, criminal intent, or under any other cause of action. You agree to accept all risks of using the information presented inside this book.

The fact that an individual or organization is referred to in this document as a citation or source of information does not imply that the author or publisher endorses the information that the individual or organization provided. This is an unofficial summary & analytical review and has not been approved by the original author of the book.

Summary of How Not To Die

Preface

In the book's preface, Dr Greger recalls how his grandmother had been diagnosed with end-stage heart disease at the age of 65, when he was a child. Having undergone multiple bypass operations by that point, her doctors told her that they could do nothing else. Soon after being discharged from the hospital, she saw a *60 Minutes* segment about Nathan Pritikin, a pioneer in the field of lifestyle medicine who had gained a reputation for his ability to reverse terminal heart disease. Dr Greger's grandmother travelled to California to sign up as one of his first patients. She signed up for his plant-based diet and graded exercise regimen, which eventually enabled her to leave her wheelchair behind and walk for up to 10 miles each day. She would live for another 31 years, and finally passed away at 96.

This experience of watching his grandmother regain her health inspired Dr Greger to pursue a career in medicine. By the time he graduated from medical school, Dean Ornish, M.D., president and founder of the non-profit Preventive Medicine Research Institute, had demonstrated that the "lowest-tech approach" (a healthy diet and lifestyle) was unequivocally effective in reversing heart disease – the nation's No. 1 killer. However, the medical industry had little incentive to address the lifestyle factors that caused such diseases. The study of nutrition has been marginalized by the medical profession, which stood to gain more financial benefits by aligning itself with the corporate interests of moneyed Big Pharma companies. He lamented the fact that his medical school curriculum only included 21 hours of nutrition training, and made no mention of the possibility of using dietary interventions as a treatment method. If he had not had the personal experience of witnessing his grandmother recovering from heart disease by making a change in her diet, his medical training would not have familiarized him with the idea using diet to prevent and treat chronic diseases.

After giving over a thousand presentations across the world, Dr Greger realised that he could disseminate the idea of diet and lifestyle interventions as a potent cure by distributing a DVD series and running a website (NutritionFacts.org). With the help of his team of researchers and volunteers, he aims to help the public digest the 24,000 medical journal articles on nutrition published each year. His ultimate goal is to "put this life-changing, life-*saving* science into practice in our daily lives", which would surely make his grandmother proud.

INTRODUCTION:

Preventing, Arresting and Reversing Our Leading Killers

Dr Greger begins the chapter by highlighting the fact that the American diet is the number one cause of premature deaths in the country, as well as the number one cause of disability. Most Americans die from diseases (especially heart attacks) rather than "old age". The common adage that "prevention is better than cure" may exist. However, the lack of emphasis on nutrition suggests that the nation's medical schools and state medical boards appear to be operating under an inverted principle: "A doctor a day may keep the apples away". The status quo revolves around the idea of treating health problems with pills, procedures and prescription drugs (an industry that is globally valued at $1 trillion annually).

The common assumption that diseases such as cancer, heart attacks, and high blood pressure are mainly attributed to genetic factors is false. The rates of these diseases mainly change when people migrate from low- to high-risk countries. For example, a Japanese American man in his forties may have the same risk for heart attack as a Japanese man in his sixties. Even if Americans are technically living longer lives than previous generations, their heavy use of prescription drugs and increased disease risk means that few of those longer years are healthy ones. Experts have even speculated that we have arrived at a time when the average youth of today will live a shorter and less healthy life than their parents.

The solution to this problem would be to embrace the idea of primordial prevention, which aims to avoid societal epidemics of chronic-disease risk factors by preventing the very factors that cause them. This is analogous to stopping people from developing high cholesterol in the first place, as opposed to helping someone with high cholesterol avoid a heart attack. The American Heart Association thus devised "The Simple 7" factors to reduce the overall incidence of heart disease:

(1) not smoking;
(2) maintaining a healthy weight;
(3) being physically active (walking for a minimum of 22 minutes each day);
(4) consuming a healthy diet (i.e. ample plants and vegetables; minimal amounts of meat and processed food);
(5) having low cholesterol levels;
(6) maintaining a normal blood pressure;
(7) keeping blood sugar at a healthy level.

When the American Heart Association's surveyed a group of 1,933 Americans, they found that only *one* individual claimed to meet all seven recommendations.

The crux of Dr Greger's argument is that our diets account for 80-90 percent of America's leading killer diseases (which will each be addressed individually in the book's subsequent chapters). Even if you are losing weight, eating smaller portions of food, and exercising regularly, you are still putting your health at risk by consuming a low-quality diet. He aims to address they "whys" for this argument in the first part of the book, and the "how" (to eat healthily) in its second part.

PART I

CHAPTER 1: *How Not to Die from Heart Disease*

Dr Greger begins the chapter by addressing the common misconception that heart disease, America's No. 1 killer, as an inevitable consequence of old age. The ground breaking China-Cornell-Oxford Project (known as the China Study) and data collected by Western-trained doctors in sub-Saharan Africa reveal that heart disease is practically non-existent among hundreds of thousands of rural Chinese villagers and millions of Africans. Immigration studies indicate that this is not due to genetic reasons. Individuals of African and Chinese descent who abandon their traditional plant-centric diets for American eating habits are certainly not exempted from high cholesterol levels and the risk of heart disease.

He also clarifies that coronary atherosclerosis can begin to develop in American children as young as ten – decades and years before they are clinically diagnosed with coronary heart disease (CHD). Even babies can be at risk if their mothers had high LDL cholesterol levels (over 150 mg/dL) throughout the pregnancy. Readers who are over ten years old should thus not only be concerned with preventing heart disease, but also with reversing the heart disease they probably already have. Since the level of elevated

LDL cholesterol in your blood is the critical risk factor for atherosclerotic plaque build-up, you should avoid all the meat, dairy and processed food products that contain it. The three main sources of LDL cholesterol are trans-fat, saturated fat, and dietary cholesterol. To be completely safe from the risk of a heart-attack, you should aim for a LDL cholesterol level that is below 70 mg/dL. The good news is that it is never too late to start reversing the build-up of plaque in your arteries by switching to a healthier diet and lifestyle.

Avoiding animal fat and animal protein is also beneficial because it reduces the amount of endotoxins you are exposed to. Endotoxins are harmful bacterial toxins that can trigger an inflammatory response in your body whether dead or alive. They cannot be destroyed even when the meat is thoroughly cooked, resulting in an inflammatory reaction in your arteries after being consumed. The food industry has lobbied hard to prevent the medical community or nutritionists from decisively labelling certain types of food as "bad" for you. Instead, they support half-truths such as claims that one can eat unhealthy foods and be healthy with sufficient exercise. After pointing out the conflict of interests between science and commerce, Dr Greger claims that replacing animal-based foods with plant-based ones is the answer. The chapter can be summed up by a quote from Neal Barnard, M.D., president of the Physicians Committee for Responsible Medicine: "Plant-based diets are the nutritional equivalent of quitting smoking".

CHAPTER 2: *How Not to Die from Lung Diseases*

Lung disease is America's No. 2 killer, taking the lives of approximately 300,000 people every year. The most fatal types of lung disease are lung cancer, chronic obstructive pulmonary disease (COPD), and asthma. As with heart disease, all three types can be mostly prevented by:

(1) not smoking; and
(2) maintaining a healthy diet.

Despite efforts by the tobacco industry to misrepresent and distort the growing body of solid scientific evidence of the dangers of smoking and inhaling second-hand smoke, the medical community has been mostly successful in firmly entrenching the negative effects of smoking in the public consciousness. The American Cancer Society has observed that your heart rate and blood pressure drops within a mere twenty minutes after quitting smoking; your blood circulation and lung function improves within a week.

Dr Greger also reveals that regular consumption of broccoli and other cruciferous vegetables has been proven to boost the activity of the detoxifying enzymes in your liver, reducing the DNA damage caused by smoking, and preventing the spread of any existing cancer to the rest of your body. Likewise, kale is singled out for its respective ability to lower bad cholesterol and boost good cholesterol levels. Meanwhile, turmeric is championed for its antioxidant and anti-carcinogenic properties. Eating these foods cannot completely reverse the negative health effects of smoking, but they can reduce them and help your body recover from the damage done.

In conclusion, the best advice for smokers, ex-smokers and non-smokers is to stay as far away from cigarettes and second-hand smoke as possible. Everyone (including those who suffer from asthma) stand to benefit from the antioxidant and anti-inflammatory effects of a diet rich in fruits and vegetables, as well as a reduction in exposure to meat's pro-oxidizing qualities.

CHAPTER 3: How Not to Die from Brain Diseases

Stroke and Alzheimer's diseases are the two most serious types of brain disease. The former kills 130,000 Americans each year, while the latter takes the lives of nearly 85,000. A stroke can claim your life instantly and quickly, but Alzheimer's takes its toll over months and years. Before you die, the amyloid plaques in your brain slowly ravage your memory and sanity.

High fiber intake is singled out as a dietary means to prevent strokes. Increasing your daily fiber intake by a mere 7 grams can reduce your risk of stroke by 7 percent. To fully protect yourself, consume at least 25 grams of soluble fiber each day, alongside 47 grams of insoluble fiber. Scientists have not fully discerned how fiber protects your brain, but they have observed how it helps control your cholesterol and blood sugar levels. This possibly reduces the amount of artery-clogging plaque in the blood vessels that nourish your brain. Consuming potassium-rich foods such as greens, beans, and sweet potatoes, oranges, and antioxidant-rich foods can also help reduce stroke risk. Getting 7-8 hours of sleep each day will have similarly beneficial effects.

As for Alzheimer's, Dr Greger points out that the medical community has arrived at the consensus that "what is good for our hearts is also good for our heads." The mental disease is thought to be largely caused by the clogging of the arteries inside of the brain with atherosclerotic plaque. As such, the plant-centric diet that staves off heart disease is also helpful in safeguarding your mental faculties. The lowest rates of Alzheimer's disease in the world can be found in rural India, where diets primarily consist of plant-based diets. Risk for the disease may increase due to genetic factors (possession of the ApoE4 gene), but the Nigerian paradox establishes the primary influence of environment over genetics. Nigerians may have the world's highest frequency of the ApoE4 allele, but they also demonstrate one of the lowest rates for the disease.

Once again, the regular consumption of a plant-based diet (particularly fruits, berries, and saffron) is key to preventing Alzheimer's and milder forms of cognitive deterioration. Meanwhile, you should also avoid all foods that contain advanced glycation end products (AGEs), which are mostly formed when high fat and protein rich foods are exposed to high temperatures (e.g. via barbequing, frying and roasting).

Finally, Dr Greger notes that regular aerobic exercise can actually reverse age-related shrinkage in your brain's memory centers by causing improvements in cerebral blood flow, memory performance, and brain tissue preservation.

CHAPTER 4: How Not to Die from Digestive Cancers

You might think that the surface of your skin is the main point of contact with the external world, but the total surface area of the folds of your gut are actually far more expansive than your skin and lungs combined. What you eat is thus likely to be your primary interface with the outside world; exposure to environmental carcinogens is very likely to occur via your diet. The three most common cancers of the digestive tract collectively kill 100,000 Americans annually. They are:

(1) Colorectal (colon and rectal) cancer;
(2) Pancreatic cancer;
(3) Esophageal cancer.

Colorectal cancer can best be prevented by regular consumption of turmeric, which is thought to be the reason for the vast discrepancy between colorectal cancer rates in the United States and India. Curcumin, the active ingredient in turmeric, is thought to reduce the number of cancer-associated structures in the rectum without causing any side effects. Colorectal cancer can also be avoided by avoiding constipation. This can be accomplished through the consumption of fiber-rich plant-based diets.

Meanwhile, research indicates that pancreatic cancer risk is significantly associated with the consumption of animal fat while no correlation was found with the consumption of plant fat. European researchers have also made a surprising finding: the daily consumption of 50 gram of chicken breast was associated with a 72 percent increased risk of pancreatic cancer. Like colorectal cancer, pancreatic cancer can be avoided by the regular consumption of curcumin-containing curries.

Finally, esophageal cancer, which occurs in the muscular tube that transports food from your mouth to your stomach, can be prevented by avoiding tobacco and alcohol. Acid reflux disease, which occurs when stomach acid inflames the inner layer of the esophagus, can also lead to esophageal cancer over time. It can be prevented by eliminating or reducing your consumption of meat and high-fat meals (especially fast food meals). On the other hand, a fiber-rich diet can help reduce your risk of developing esophageal cancer by 50 percent. On the other hand, a fiber-rich diet can help reduce your risk of developing esophageal cancer by 50 percent.

CHAPTER 5: How Not to Die from Infections

The recent health scares of mad cow disease and swine flu are surfaced early on in the chapter, as a grave reminder that "nearly three-quarters of all emerging and re-emerging human diseases arise from the animal kingdom". This includes diseases such as tuberculosis (from domesticated goats), measles and smallpox (from mutant cattle viruses), whooping cough (from domesticated pigs), typhoid fever (from domesticated chickens), influenza (from domesticated ducks), cold virus (from horses) and HIV (from African primates). Exotic diseases such as SARS or Ebola may capture the headlines, but most people with infections die of the most common ones such as influenza and pneumonia. Exposure to them may be inevitable; we should safeguard our immune system and practice good hygiene to protect our health.

A few fruits and vegetables are singled out for their ability to boost our immune system: kale, broccoli, berries (especially blueberries), probiotics, chlorella, and mushrooms. Dr Greger also notes that exercise has been proven to boost the ability of your immune systems to fight infections.

On the other side of the coin, food poisoning can best be avoided by staying clear of devastating pathogen food combinations such as poultry (meat and eggs) with *Campylobacter* and *Salmonella* bacteria, pork with *Yersinia* bacteria and *Toxoplasma* parasites, and deli meats and dairy products with *Listeria* bacteria. Besides possibly exposing yourself to these various pathogens when you consume meat products, you also risk consuming the antibiotic residues caused by the over-prescription of antibiotics to farm animals.

CHAPTER 6: *How Not to Die from Diabetes*

Type 2 Diabetes has been described as the "Black Death of the twenty-first century" for its spread and devastating health effects across the globe. Over 20 million Americans have been diagnosed with diabetes, and one in three Americans may become diabetic by 2050. The risk factors for diabetes include:

(1) insulin resistance, which is aggravated by high fat diets;
(2) childhood obesity;
(3) the possession of excessive body fat.

Thankfully, Type 2 diabetes is nearly always preventable, typically treatable, and occasionally reversible via diet and lifestyle improvements.

Research has revealed that plant-rich diets help protect against diabetes, even when the individuals studied were of the same weight. When compared to omnivores, vegans had less amounts of fat in their muscles, better insulin sensitivity, better blood sugar levels, better levels of insulins and better functioning beta cells (the pancreatic cells that produce insulin). In particular, the consumption of large amounts of legumes (e.g., beans, split peas, chickpeas, and lentils) has been liked to better blood sugar levels, improved cholesterol and better insulin regulation. Furthermore, the consumption of larger amounts of fruits and vegetables helps you feel satiated easily without consuming ample amounts of calories.

Meanwhile, saturated fats have been proven to be detrimental to your beta cells. When the health outcomes of healthy omnivores and vegetarians were compared, the vegetarians had significantly lower risks of both prediabetes and diabetes. Dr Greger argues that adopting a plant-based diet is preferable to voluntary calorie restriction or surgery. All you have to do is adopt a diet that revolved around whole plant foods.

CHAPTER 7: How Not to Die from High Blood Pressure

After combing through nearly one hundred thousand data sources, the Global Burden of Disease Study (which was funded by the Bill & Melinda Gates Foundation) identified high blood pressure as the No. 1 risk factor for death in the world. Nine million lives worldwide are claimed each year, from associated causes such as aneurysms, heart attacks, heart failure, kidney failure, and stroke. High blood pressure strains not only the heart, but also crucial blood vessels in the eyes, kidneys and brain.

The high incidences of high blood pressure in the Western world and developing nations are certainly not genetic. The main culprit is an excessive sodium intake, which can be traced back to the processed food industry, cheese, pizza, saltshakers on the dinner table, and chicken (the poultry industry routinely injects chicken carcasses with salt water to artificially increase their weight and selling price). Regular overconsumption of salt dulls your taste buds, causing your to crave even greater amounts of salt in your food. Avoiding hyper-salty processed foods and excessive amounts of salt in your cooking is thus crucial to reducing your risk of high blood pressure.

On the flipside, consumption of the following foods can reduce the risk of hypertension:

(1) whole grains;

(2) flaxseeds;

(3) hibiscus tea;

(4) nitrate-rich vegetables such as beets, Swiss chard, oak leaf lettuce, beet greens, basil, butter leaf lettuce, rhubarb, and arugula.

CHAPTER 8: How Not to Die from Liver Diseases

Some forms of liver disease such as iron-overload disease hemochromatosis are inherited, but the major of liver disease incidents that kill 60,000 Americans each year are alcoholic liver disease and fatty liver disease. Both are caused by the abuse of drink and food and are fully preventable.

Alcohol is the third leading killer in the United States of America. Alcohol-related deaths are divided equally between motor vehicle accidents and alcoholic liver disease. The latter is caused by the accumulation of liver fat due to excessive consumption of alcohol. When men drink more than two drinks a day and women drink more than one drink per day, they put themselves at risk for inflammation, liver scarring and eventual liver failure. With regard to the common assumption that moderate drinking can be beneficial to one's health, Dr Greger argues that that is only true for those who "fail to practice a bare modicum of healthy behaviors".

On the other hand, non-alcoholic fatty liver disease (NAFLD) occurs when fat deposits accumulate in the liver due to the consumption of excessive amounts of calories, animal fat, cholesterol, sugar, and fast food. Viral hepatitis (hepatitis A, B, C, D and E), another common cause of liver disease, can be avoided by vaccination, staying clear of raw and semi-cooked shellfish, and practicing good hygiene.

Dr Greger recommends the following foods to protect your liver:

(1) oatmeal (a bowl per day);
(2) cranberries (in the form of a cocktail of fresh or frozen cranberries);
(3) coffee (not more than four cups per day).

CHAPTER 9: How Not to Die from Blood Cancers

Blood cancers typically occur due to mutations in your white blood cells. They can be categorized into leukemia, lymphoma, and myeloma. Fortunately, dietary changes may reduce our risk of all these blood cancers. While blood cancers claim thousands of American lives each year, you can you reduce your risk of suffering from them by making key dietary changes.

Researchers are still pursuing the exact biochemical mechanisms behind the anti-carcinogenic effects of plant-based diets, which have been found to protect against leukemia, lymphoma, and multiple myeloma. Cruciferous vegetables such as broccoli, cauliflower, kale, collard greens, watercress, bok choy, kohlrabi, rutabaga, turnips, arugula, radishes (including horseradish), wasabi, and all types of cabbage have been found to be particularly protective against blood cancers. Other beneficial foods include acai berries, turmeric, purple cabbage, cloves and cinnamon.

Dr Greger ends the chapter by arguing that actively avoiding animal products is also crucial in reducing your risk of blood cancer. Researchers have found that eating even small amounts of poultry significantly increases your risk for lymphoma and leukemia. Workers in the livestock and meatpacking industries who are heavily exposed to cattle and pigs suffer from a greater risk of non-Hodgkin's lymphoma. Scientists are still unpacking the role that tumor-promoting farm animal viruses play in causing human cancers.

CHAPTER 10: How Not to Die from Kidney Disease

When your kidneys begin to malfunction, the metabolic waste products that should be excreted via urine begin to build up in your blood. This can lead to a shortness of breath, abnormal heart rhythms, confusion and feeling weak. Kidney malfunction and failure can be caused by exposure to particular toxins, infections or urinary blockage. However, most kidney diseases involve a slow diminishment of function over time and can be prevented by adopting a diet built around unprocessed plant foods. Purple and red cabbage are singled out for their ability to balance out the acidity of the average Western diet, which significantly increases your risk of developing kidney stones.

Furthermore, the foods that damage and cause an additional burden on your kidneys should be avoided. Researchers have discovered three dietary components that are associated with reduced kidney function: animal protein, animal fat and cholesterol. The medical community has accepted the concept of lipid nephrotoxicity, which is based on the notion that excessive levels of fat and cholesterol in the bloodstream are potentially toxic to the kidneys. In addition, high levels of animal protein consumption have been found to dramatically increase the kidney's workload, inducing a high-stress state of hyper filtration. Finally, animal protein consumption also increases your dietary acid load, which elevates the risk of protein leakage into urine and eventually leads to kidney damage.

CHAPTER 11: How Not to Die from Breast Cancer

Breast cancer is a gradual disease that can build up over decades, as a single cancer cell multiplies into a tiny tumor which then grows in size. By the time the tumor can be detected by modern technology, a woman is likely to have been hosting the cancerous cells for two decades. Therefore, adopting an anti-cancerous diet and lifestyle is preventive of the initiation *and* promotion stage of cancer (when there are enough cancerous cells to pose a threat).

The American Institute for Cancer Research (AICR) has advocated for the following lifestyle changes to prevent the often-fatal disease:

(1) avoiding tobacco;
(2) limiting alcohol consumption;
(3) maintaining a normal body weight;
(4) consuming a diet that is rich in vegetables, whole grains, fruits and beans.

Consuming a plant-rich diet and walking daily can improve your defenses against cancer in only two weeks. Moderate consumption of red wine has been found to reduce the risk of breast cancer, but you can access its benefits by consuming grape juice, purple grapes, strawberries, apples (do not discard the peel, which contains the most antioxidants), broccoli, green tea, flaxseeds, soy products, pomegranates and plain white mushrooms. You can also benefit from uninterrupted sleep at night, reducing your meat intake, consuming adequate fiber, and exercising regularly.

CHAPTER 12: How Not to Die from Suicidal Depression

Major depression is the category of mental illness is that is most often diagnosed. It affects approximately 7 percent of American adults, causing "the blues" as well as weight gain or loss, fatigue, a weaker immune system and difficulties in concentrating. Though there are many factors that contribute to incidences of mental illness, Dr Gundry argues that exposure to particular foods and avoidance of others can improve the odds for your mental health.

Researchers have argued that the pro-inflammatory compound of arachidonic acid – which is found in chicken, eggs, beef, pork, and fish - can "adversely impact mental health via a cascade of neuro-inflammation". In contrast, a greater consumption of vegetables has been associated with a 62 percent decrease in the risk of developing depression. Furthermore, the levels of the enzyme called monoamine oxidase (known as MAO, it controls neurotransmitters such as serotonin and dopamine) – which are elevated in depressed individuals – can be reduced by the consumption of plant foods such as apples, berries, grapes, onions, green tea and spices such as oregano, cloves, cinnamon and nutmeg. You can also benefit from the consumption of seeds (e.g. sesame, sunflower, or pumpkin), saffron, coffee (avoid sugar and artificial sweeteners when drinking), and anti-oxidant-rich plant foods (particularly tomatoes).

CHAPTER 13: How Not to Die from Prostate Cancer

Like the glandular tissue in the human breast, the glandular tissue in the prostate can become cancerous. Over half of the male population above the age of eighty have prostate cancer. Although prostate cancer may not cause any harm even if undetected, almost 28,000 die each year due to the disease.

Dr Greger observes that cow's milk – which is designed to help calves rapidly gain weight – has been associated with various cancers. In particular, the consumption of dairy products such as milk, low-fat milk, and cheese appear to increase your total prostate cancer risk. The presence of cooked-meat carcinogens in chicken and turkey and the choline in eggs have also been associated with a greater risk of dying from prostate cancer.

You can thankfully suppress and reverse the growth of prostate cancer cells by adopting plant-based diet. Consuming cruciferous vegetables (broccoli, Brussel sprouts, cabbage, cauliflower, or kale), flaxseed, garlic, onions, and legumes (beans, chickpeas, split peas, and lentils) will be particularly conducive towards maintaining good prostate health.

CHAPTER 14: How Not to Die from Parkinson's Disease

Parkinson's disease, the most common neurodegenerative disease after Alzheimer's, is not presently curable. It robs your speed, quality and ease of movement. Besides causing the hallmark hand tremors, limb stiffness, and impaired balance, it also adversely affects your mood, your ability to think and your ability to sleep. Professional athletes who suffer from a history of head trauma are at a greater risk of developing Parkinson's. Most people, however, stand to develop it from exposure to the toxic pollutants in our food supply and environment (e.g. heavy metals, banned pesticides, and chemicals from plastics). We face the greatest risk of exposure to heavy metals from poultry and tuna (arsenic), dairy (lead), and seafood (mercury).

Though it may be impossible to avoid all the pollutants and pesticides in our environment, you can still improve your odds by eating more plants – which have the lowest possible exposure to industrial toxins on the food chain. Individuals who subsist wholly on plant-based diets benefit from lower levels of pollutants, pesticides and chemicals which have been associated with neurological problems. The following foods are recommended for their protective properties: blueberries, strawberries, coffee, peppers, and green tea.

CHAPTER 15: *How Not to Die from Iatrogenic Causes (or, How Not to Die from Doctors)*

In this chapter, Dr Greger argues that modern medicine can be counterproductive when dealing with chronic diseases (while excelling at treating broken bones and curing infections). The side effects from medications provided in hospitals alone contributed to the deaths of 106,000 Americans per annum. Other causes of death include:

(1) being provided the wrong medication by error – 7,000 deaths;
(2) hospital errors – 20,000 deaths;
(3) hospital-acquired infections – 99,000 deaths;
(4) complications due to surgeries – 12,000 deaths).

Despite warnings about the dangers of overworked nurses, interns and doctors, fatal fatigue-related medical errors continue to occur.

To avoid becoming another casualty to the carelessness of modern hospitals, Dr Greger suggests that you should avoid getting sick in the first place. He makes the following recommendations to achieve this goal:

(1) reducing your risk of radiation exposure by avoiding unnecessary CT scans and airplane flights, and consuming ginger, lemon balm tea;

(2) opting for a healthy enough diet instead of a regimen of prescription drugs;

(3) avoiding unnecessary colonoscopies, which may be killing thousands of Americans each year.

PART II

INTRODUCTION

The second part of the book addresses a common question often posed to Dr Greger: "What do *you* eat every day, Dr. Greger?" It includes two simple tools to integrate his scientific research into your everyday life:

(1) The "Traffic Light" system which helps you to quickly identify the healthiest options;
(2) The Daily Dozen checklist that makes it easy for you to include his "essential foods" into your everyday diet.

In general, the aim is to avoid sugars, calories, cholesterol, saturated fat, sodium, and trans fat while maximizing intake of fiber, the minerals calcium, magnesium, and potassium, and vitamins A, C, D, E, and K.

The Traffic Light system consists of:

- "Red" foods (ultra-processed plant foods and processed animal foods, which are to be avoided;
- "Yellow" foods (processed plant foods and unprocessed animal foods, which are to be consumed sparingly);

- "Green" foods (unprocessed plant foods).

Dr Greger notes that there are instances of processed plant foods being healthier (e.g. tomato juice), and thus defines "unprocessed" as "nothing bad added, nothing good taken away". In general, however, unprocessed foods are healthier than their processed counterparts, even if a processed food product (e.g. almond milk) is not necessarily bad for your health. Instead of thinking of your diet in terms of what you exclude (i.e. as vegans or vegetarians), he recommends that you think of it in terms of what you mostly consume (which should be unprocessed plant foods).

SUMMARY OF HOW NOT TO DIE

Dr Greger's Daily Dozen

After making a disclaimer that he would "rather just present the science and let others decide for themselves on what they eat each day", Dr Greger presents the list of foods that he tries to incorporate into his daily diet:

(1) Three servings of beans

- Legumes such as beans, lentils, tempeh and soy products are a special category of food because they contain protein, iron and zinc alongside the nutrients found in the vegetable kingdom (fiber, folate, and potassium). Tempeh is a whole soy food, and thus preferable to tofu.
- They can be eaten for breakfast in the form of baked beans, miso soup, idli, edamame, or hummus.

(2) One serving of berries

- Antioxidant-rich berries protect against cancer, boost your immune system while guarding your liver.
- Blackberries have the most antioxidants (650 units), followed by blueberries (380), cranberries (330), and strawberries (310 units).
- Most of the nutrition provided by berries will be retained after freezing but lost when they are turned into jam.

- Frozen berries can be used to make "instant all-fruit ice cream" via a blender, food processor, or juicer.

(3) Three servings of other fruits
- Can be consumed raw, cooked (e.g. baked apples, poached pears, and grilled pineapple), or blended.
- Avoid juicing fruits since the fiber is eliminated this way.
- Make your own dried fruit with a dehydrator, since there is often added sugar in store-bought dried fruits.

(4) One serving of cruciferous vegetables
- Obtain the full nutrients of broccoli, Brussels sprouts, kale, collards, cauliflower, or any other cruciferous vegetable by chopping them up and then waiting for forty minutes before cooking.
- Cauliflower and broccoli can be mashed or roasted.
- Kale chips are actually healthy.

(5) Two servings of greens
- Use "flavor-flavor" conditioning to make vegetables more palatable if you find the bitter taste intolerable (e.g. adding balsamic vinegar or sweet fruits into a green smoothie).
- Boiling greens are fine if you are making soup since the nutrients dissolved in the water will not be lost.

- Vinegar makes a great salad dressing due to its anti-glycemic effect.

(6) Two servings of other vegetables

- Diversify your vegetable consumption by branching out to include root vegetables like sweet potatoes, stem vegetables like rhubarb, pod vegetables like peas, and flower vegetables like broccoli.
- Consume mushrooms, since they contain ergothioneine – a potent intra-mitochondrial antioxidant.
- Try roasting vegetables (peppers, okra, Brussels sprouts, beets, or squash) if you do not like their normal texture.
- Cauliflower, Brussels sprouts, green onion, leek, and garlic are particularly effective against cancer.
- The nutrient profile of carrots and celery stalks improve via cooking, while artichokes, beets, and onions retain 97.5% of their antioxidant power.

(7) One serving of flaxseeds

- Flaxseeds can be eaten whole.
- Ground flax can be sprinkled on salads, soups, or oatmeal.

(8) One serving of nuts

- Nuts can be eaten as snacks, or blended into sauces and consumed with vegetables.
- Nuts can also be consumed as soups, e.g. African peanut stew.

(9) One serving of spices

- Cooked turmeric seems to offer better DNA protection, while raw turmeric may have greater anti-inflammatory effects (so consume them in both ways).
- Turmeric can easily be found in Indian and Moroccan cuisines.
- Other spices include powdered fenugreek seed, cilantro, ginger, peppermint, and cayenne pepper.

(10) Three servings of whole grains

- Apart from whole wheat bread, oatmeal and brown rice, try quinoa, kañiwa and fonio.
- When buying processed grain products, use the "Five-to-One Rule" to see if the ratio of grams of carbohydrates to grams of dietary fiber is five or less.

(11) Five servings of beverages

- Try adding fresh fruit or veggies to water to make it less boring.

- Coffee (when drunk in moderation) has some health benefits.
- Green tea has been proven to possess more potent health effects.
- Hibiscus tea has some of the highest antioxidant concentrations.

(12) One "serving" of exercise
- This can be in the form of 90 minutes of moderate-intensity activity or 40 minutes of vigorous activity.
- Apart from incorporating more physical activity, switching to a standing desk if your job involves hours of sitting down for more than 6 hours per day.

He then presents a short chapter on each component of the daily dozen, which includes the specific types of food, cooking methods, serving sizes, disclaimers, exceptions and additional considerations.

Conclusion

As the book ends, Dr Greger notes that "How Not to Die" can be considered as a strange book title, since everyone has to die at some point. He clarifies that the book's goal is to prevent you from dying *prematurely*. This goal can be achieved by actively taking responsibility for your health, adopting a strictly plant-based diet, and learning to ignore the machinations of the food industries, which aim to hijack your dopamine reward system for corporate profit.

Background Information about How Not to Die

How Not to Die: Discover the Foods Scientifically Proven to Prevent and Reverse Disease was written by Dr Michael Greger with the help of Gene Stone. It draws from Dr Greger's professional experience as a noted lecturer, physician and the founder of NutritionFacts.org. It was published in December 2016 by Flatiron Books, and became a *New York Times* bestseller. At 576 pages, it serves as a tome of evidence that make the case for a whole foods and plant-based diet. The first half of the book focuses on how the fifteen main killers in America (e.g. heart disease, high blood pressure, diabetes, and various cancers) can be avoided by adopting a healthier diet and lifestyle. The second half provides additional scientific details and practical advice on how to incorporate the healthiest foods into your daily meals. The book is also noteworthy for its critical stance towards prescription pills, pharmaceutical and surgical approaches to chronic diseases, and the conflict of interest between Big Pharma, Big Food and the general wellbeing of the population.

While his peers generally agree with his overarching message of avoiding animal products and processed foods in favor of wide range of minimally processed plant foods, they have expressed some skepticism about overstating the ability of plant consumption to combat various types of diseases[1]. Denise Minger, a popular nutrition writer, has argued that the book "paints nutritional science with a

---

[1] https://www.psychologytoday.com/blog/looking-in-the-cultural-mirror/201605/how-not-die

broad, suspiciously uncomplicated brush[2]". Minger has pointed out that Dr Greger cherry-picked scientific studies to support his main thesis, and thus understated the beneficial effects of moderate meat and seafood consumption.

---

[2] https://www.healthline.com/nutrition/how-not-to-die-review

Background Information about Dr Michael Greger

Dr Michael Greger graduated from the Cornell University School of Agriculture and Tufts University School of Medicine, and is a general practitioner that specializes in clinical nutrition. He is a founding member and Fellow of the American College of Lifestyle Medicine, as well as an internationally renowned speaker on the topics of nutrition, food safety and public health issues. He is the founder of NutritionFacts.org, a "strictly non-commercial, science-based public service" that provides the public with updates on the latest developments in nutrition research in bite-sized videos. Prior to this, he raised awareness about the dangers mad cow disease and criticized the Atkins diet.

His two recent books, *How Not to Die* and the *How Not to Die Cookbook* were instant New York Times Best Sellers. In 2017, he received the ACLM Lifestyle Medicine Trailblazer Award and was appointed as a diplomat of the American Board of Lifestyle Medicine.

Cover Questions

1. Why does Dr Greger prefer the dietary advice published by the American Institute for Cancer Research (AICR) over the dietary guidelines provided by the U.S. Department of Agriculture (USDA)?

2. What is wrong with the idea of eating whatever you want and then taking the appropriate medications when health complications emerge?

3. How does Dr Greger define "unprocessed" foods?

Trivia Questions about How Not to Die

1. Why is the Standard American Diet so "sad"?

2. Which deadly diseases do cruciferous vegetables help protect you against?

3. Which components of traditional Indian diets have been credited for the low incidents of heart disease within the subcontinent?

4. Why is fiber consumption so important?

5. Why should you avoid meat and meat-derived products that have been exposed to dry-heat cooking methods?

6. Why does stool size matter?

7. What is Dr Greger's general stance on using health supplements for better health?

8. Does the common saying "too much of a good thing" apply to the consumption of unprocessed plant foods?

Trivia Questions about Dr Michael Greger

1. Why does Dr Greger warn readers about making dietary decisions based on his (well-informed) personal choices?

2. Which pivotal childhood incident inspired Dr Greger to pursue a career in medicine?

3. How would you describe Dr Greger's attitude towards Big Pharma and Big Food?

4. Who are the nutrition and medicine thought leaders that Dr Greger looks up to?

5. What are the types of disease(s) that have plagued some of Dr Greger's family members?

Discussion Questions

1. Do you have any family members who have struggled with some of the fatal diseases described in the book?

2. What are some of the diseases that begin to affect us from a very young age?

3. Why do some vegetarians and vegans fail to benefit from reduced risks of chronic diseases?

4. Why do you think Americans perform so poorly in meeting their daily requirements of fruit and vegetables?

5. How many of the "The Simple 7" factors advocated by the American Heart Association apply to your lifestyle?

6. Is the phrase "A doctor a day may keep the apples away" an accurate metaphor for modern medicine?

7. Is a heart healthy diet also a brain healthy diet?

8. What are telomeres, and how does your diet affect them?

9. What are some of the recommended ways of eating the Dr Greger's favourite vegetables?

10. How has the business aspect of medicine compromised its practice?

Thank You

We hope that you've enjoyed your reading experience.

Here at Concise Reading, we will always strive to deliver to you the highest quality guides.

We'd like to thank you for supporting us and reading until the very end.

Before you go, would you mind leaving us a review on Amazon?

It will mean a lot to us and help us continue to create high quality guides for you in the future.

Warmly yours,

The Concise Reading Team

Made in the USA
Middletown, DE
22 April 2018